100 BEST Hamburger RECIPES

Publications International, Ltd.
Favorite Brand Name Recipes at www.fbnr.com

Pictured on the front cover: Suzie's Sloppy Joes *(page 36).*

Pictured on the back cover *(clockwise from top left):* Mexican Taco Salad *(page 38),* Silly Spaghetti Casserole *(page 67),* Mama's Best Ever Spaghetti & Meatballs *(page 20)* and Crunchy Layered Beef & Bean Salad *(page 113).*

ISBN-13: 978-1-4127-9655-2
ISBN-10: 1-4127-9655-5

Manufactured in China.

8 7 6 5 4 3 2 1

Microwave Cooking: Microwave ovens vary in wattage. Use the cooking times as guidelines and check for doneness before adding more time.

Preparation/Cooking Times: Preparation times are based on the approximate amount of time required to assemble the recipe before cooking, baking, chilling or serving. These times include preparation steps such as measuring, chopping and mixing. The fact that some preparations and cooking can be done simultaneously is taken into account. Preparation of optional ingredients and serving suggestions is not included.

Contents

Hamburger
CLASSICS

Hearty Nachos

1 pound ground beef
1 envelope LIPTON® RECIPE SECRETS® Onion Soup Mix
1 can (19 ounces) black beans, rinsed and drained
1 cup prepared salsa
1 package (8½ ounces) plain tortilla chips
1 cup shredded Cheddar cheese (about 4 ounces)

1. In 12-inch nonstick skillet, brown ground beef over medium-high heat; drain.

2. Stir in soup mix, black beans and salsa. Bring to a boil over high heat. Reduce heat to low and simmer 5 minutes or until heated through.

3. Arrange tortilla chips on serving platter. Spread beef mixture over chips; sprinkle with Cheddar cheese. Top, if desired, with sliced green onions, sliced pitted ripe olives, chopped tomato and chopped cilantro.

Makes 8 servings

Prep Time: 10 minutes
Cook Time: 12 minutes

Heartland Shepherd's Pie

¾ **pound ground beef**
1 **medium onion, chopped**
1 **can (14½ ounces) DEL MONTE® Original Recipe Stewed Tomatoes**
1 **can (8 ounces) DEL MONTE Tomato Sauce**
1 **can (14½ ounces) DEL MONTE Mixed Vegetables, drained**
   Instant mashed potato flakes plus ingredients to prepare (enough for 6 servings)
3 **cloves garlic, minced (optional)**

1. Preheat oven to 375°F. In large skillet, brown meat and onion over medium-high heat; drain.

2. Add tomatoes and tomato sauce; cook over high heat until thickened, stirring frequently. Stir in mixed vegetables. Season with salt and pepper, if desired.

3. Spoon into 2-quart baking dish; set aside. Prepare 6 servings mashed potatoes according to package directions, first cooking garlic in specified amount of butter.

4. Top meat mixture with potatoes. Bake 20 minutes or until heated through. Garnish with chopped parsley, if desired.

Makes 4 to 6 servings

Prep Time: 5 minutes
Cook Time: 30 minutes

Heartland Shepherd's Pie

Backyard Barbecue Burgers

1½ pounds ground beef
⅓ cup barbecue sauce, divided
1 onion, peeled and sliced
1 to 2 tomatoes, sliced
1 to 2 tablespoons olive oil
6 kaiser rolls, split
   Green or red leaf lettuce

1. Prepare grill for direct grilling. Combine ground beef and 2 tablespoons barbecue sauce in large bowl. Shape into six 1-inch-thick patties.

2. Place patties on grid directly above medium-hot coals. Grill, uncovered, until no longer pink in center (160°F), turning and brushing often with remaining barbecue sauce.

3. Meanwhile, brush onion and tomato slices with oil.* Place on grid. Grill onion slices about 10 minutes and tomato slices about 2 to 3 minutes.

4. Just before serving, place rolls, cut side down, on grid and grill until toasted. Serve patties on toasted rolls with grilled onions, tomatoes and lettuce.   *Makes 6 servings*

Onion slices may also be cooked in 2 tablespoons oil in large skillet over medium heat 10 minutes until tender and slightly brown.

Backyard Barbecue Burger

Southwestern Meat Loaf

1 envelope LIPTON® RECIPE SECRETS® Onion Soup Mix*
2 pounds ground beef
2 cups (about 3 ounces) cornflakes or bran flakes cereal, crushed
1½ cups frozen or drained canned whole kernel corn
1 small green bell pepper, chopped
2 eggs
¾ cup water
⅓ cup ketchup

Also terrific with LIPTON® RECIPE SECRETS® Onion-Mushroom or Beefy Onion Soup Mix.

1. Preheat oven to 350°F. In large bowl, combine all ingredients.

2. In 13×9-inch baking or roasting pan, shape into loaf.

3. Bake uncovered 1 hour or until done. Let stand 10 minutes before serving. Serve, if desired, with salsa.   *Makes 8 servings*

Recipe Tip: For a great lunchbox treat, wrap leftover meat loaf slices in a tortilla and top with your favorite taco toppings such as salsa, sour cream, grated cheese and shredded lettuce.

Southwestern Meat Loaf

Chili-Stuffed Poblano Peppers

1 pound lean ground beef
4 large poblano peppers
1 can (15 ounces) chili-seasoned beans
1 can (14½ ounces) chili-style chunky tomatoes, undrained
1 tablespoon Mexican (Adobo) seasoning
⅔ cup shredded Mexican cheese blend or Monterey Jack cheese

1. Preheat broiler. Bring 2 quarts water to a boil in 3-quart saucepan. Brown beef in large nonstick skillet 6 to 8 minutes over medium-high heat, stirring to break up meat. Drain fat.

2. Meanwhile, cut peppers in half lengthwise; remove stems and seeds. Add 4 pepper halves to boiling water; cook 3 minutes or until bright green and slightly softened. Remove and drain upside down on plate. Repeat with remaining 4 halves. Set aside.

3. Add beans, tomatoes and Mexican seasoning to ground beef. Cook and stir over medium heat 5 minutes or until mixture thickens slightly.

4. Arrange peppers, cut side up, in 13×9-inch baking dish. Divide chili mixture evenly among each pepper; top with cheese. Broil 6 inches from heat 1 minute or until cheese is melted. Serve immediately.

Makes 4 servings

Serving Suggestion: Serve with cornbread and chunky salsa.

Prep and Cook Time: 26 minutes

Chili-Stuffed Poblano Pepper

Special Occasion Meat Loaf

    1 pound ground beef
    1 pound Italian sausage, removed from casings and crumbled
 1½ cups seasoned bread crumbs
    2 eggs, lightly beaten
    2 tablespoons chopped fresh parsley
    2 cloves garlic, minced
    1 teaspoon salt
  ½ teaspoon black pepper
    2 cups water
    1 tablespoon butter
    1 package (about 4 ounces) Spanish rice mix
    2 packages (10 ounces each) frozen chopped spinach, thawed and
      well drained

1. Combine ground beef, sausage, bread crumbs, eggs, parsley, garlic, salt and pepper in large bowl; mix well. Place on 12×12-inch sheet of foil moistened with water. Cover with 14×12-inch sheet of waxed paper moistened with water. Press meat mixture into 12×12-inch square with hands or rolling pin. Refrigerate 2 hours or until well chilled.

2. Bring water, butter and rice mix to a boil in medium saucepan. Continue boiling over medium heat 10 minutes or until rice is tender, stirring occasionally. Refrigerate 2 hours or until well chilled.

3. Preheat oven to 350°F. Remove waxed paper from ground beef mixture. Spread spinach over ground beef mixture, leaving 1-inch border. Spread rice evenly over spinach. Starting at one side, roll up jelly-roll style, using foil as a guide; removing foil while rolling. Seal edges tightly. Place meat loaf seam side down in 13×9-inch baking pan. Bake, uncovered, about 1 hour. Let stand 15 minutes before serving. Cut into 1-inch slices.   *Makes about 8 servings*

Lasagna Supreme

8 ounces uncooked lasagna noodles
½ pound ground beef
½ pound mild Italian sausage, casings removed
1 medium onion, chopped
2 cloves garlic, minced
1 can (14½ ounces) whole peeled tomatoes, undrained, chopped
1 can (6 ounces) tomato paste
2 teaspoons dried basil
1 teaspoon dried marjoram
1 can (4 ounces) sliced mushrooms, drained
2 eggs
2 cups (16 ounces) cream-style cottage cheese
¾ cup grated Parmesan cheese, divided
2 tablespoons dried parsley flakes
½ teaspoon salt
½ teaspoon black pepper
2 cups (8 ounces) shredded Cheddar cheese
3 cups (12 ounces) shredded mozzarella cheese

1. Cook lasagna noodles according to package directions; drain. Cook meats, onion and garlic in large skillet over medium-high heat until meat is brown, stirring to separate meat. Drain fat.

2. Add tomatoes with juice, tomato paste, basil and marjoram. Reduce heat to low. Cover; simmer 15 minutes, stirring often. Stir in mushrooms; set aside.

3. Preheat oven to 375°F. Beat eggs in large bowl; add cottage cheese, ½ cup Parmesan cheese, parsley, salt and pepper. Mix well.

4. Place half the noodles in bottom of greased 13×9-inch baking pan. Spread half the cottage cheese mixture over noodles, then half the meat mixture and half the Cheddar cheese and mozzarella cheese. Repeat layers. Top with remaining ¼ cup Parmesan cheese.

5. Bake lasagna 40 to 45 minutes or until bubbly. Let stand 10 minutes before cutting. *Makes 8 to 10 servings*

Lipton® Onion Burgers

1 envelope LIPTON® RECIPE SECRETS® Onion Soup Mix*
2 pounds ground beef
½ cup water

Also terrific with LIPTON® RECIPE SECRETS® Beefy Onion, Onion Mushroom, Beefy Mushroom, Savory Herb with Garlic or Ranch Soup Mix.

1. In large bowl, combine all ingredients; shape into 8 patties.

2. Grill or broil until done.   *Makes about 8 servings*

Prep Time: 10 minutes
Cook Time: 12 minutes

Kid's Choice Meatballs

1½ pounds ground beef
¼ cup dry seasoned bread crumbs
¼ cup grated Parmesan cheese
3 tablespoons *French's®* Worcestershire Sauce
1 egg
2 jars (14 ounces *each*) spaghetti sauce

1. Preheat oven to 425°F. In bowl, gently mix beef, bread crumbs, cheese, Worcestershire and egg. Shape into 1-inch meatballs. Place on rack in roasting pan. Bake 15 minutes or until cooked.

2. In large saucepan, combine meatballs and spaghetti sauce. Cook until heated through. Serve over cooked pasta.
                    Makes 6 to 8 servings (about 48 meatballs)

Quick Meatball Tip: On waxed paper, pat meat mixture into 8×6×1-inch rectangle. With knife, cut crosswise and lengthwise into 1-inch rows. Roll each small square into a ball.

Prep Time: 10 minutes
Cook Time: 20 minutes

Lipton® Onion Burgers

Original Ortega® Taco Recipe

  1 pound ground beef
¾ cup water
  1 package (1¼ ounces) ORTEGA® Taco Seasoning Mix
  1 package (12) ORTEGA® Taco Shells, warmed
    Toppings: shredded lettuce, chopped tomatoes, shredded mild
      Cheddar cheese, ORTEGA® Thick & Smooth Taco Sauce

BROWN beef; drain. Stir in water and seasoning mix. Bring to a boil. Reduce heat to low; cook, stirring occasionally, for 5 to 6 minutes or until mixture is thickened.

FILL taco shells with beef mixture. Top with lettuce, tomatoes, cheese and taco sauce. *Makes 6 servings*

Classic Hamburger Casserole

  1 pound ground beef
  1 package (9 ounces) frozen cut green beans, thawed and drained
  1 can (10¾ ounces) condensed tomato soup
¼ cup water
½ teaspoon seasoned salt
⅛ teaspoon pepper
  2 cups hot mashed potatoes
1⅓ cups *French's*® French Fried Onions, divided
½ cup (2 ounces) shredded Cheddar cheese

Preheat oven to 350°F. In medium skillet, brown ground beef; drain. Stir in green beans, soup, water and seasonings; pour into 1½-quart casserole. In medium bowl, combine mashed potatoes and ⅔ cup French Fried Onions. Spoon potato mixture in mounds around edge of casserole. Bake, uncovered, at 350°F for 25 minutes or until heated through. Top potatoes with cheese and remaining ⅔ cup onions; bake, uncovered, 5 minutes or until onions are golden brown.
Makes 4 to 6 servings

Original Ortega® Taco Recipe

Mama's Best Ever
Spaghetti & Meatballs

1 pound lean ground beef
½ cup Italian seasoned dry bread crumbs
1 egg
1 jar (26 to 28 ounces) RAGÚ® Old World Style® Pasta Sauce
8 ounces spaghetti, cooked and drained

1. In medium bowl, combine ground beef, bread crumbs and egg; shape into 12 meatballs.

2. In 3-quart saucepan, bring Ragú Pasta Sauce to a boil over medium-high heat. Gently stir in meatballs.

3. Reduce heat to low and simmer covered, stirring occasionally, 20 minutes or until meatballs are no longer pink in centers. Serve over hot spaghetti; sprinkle with shredded Parmesan cheese, if desired. *Makes 4 servings*

Prep Time: 10 minutes
Cook Time: 20 minutes

Mama's Best Ever
Spaghetti & Meatballs

Pizza Meat Loaf

    1 envelope LIPTON® RECIPE SECRETS® Onion Soup Mix*
    2 pounds ground beef
 1½ cups fresh bread crumbs
    2 eggs
    1 small green bell pepper, chopped (optional)
  ¼ cup water
    1 cup RAGÚ® OLD WORLD STYLE® Pasta Sauce, divided
    1 cup shredded mozzarella cheese (about 4 ounces), divided

*Also terrific with LIPTON® RECIPE SECRETS® Savory Herb with Garlic Soup Mix.

1. Preheat oven to 350°F. In large bowl, combine all ingredients except ½ cup pasta sauce and ½ cup cheese.

2. In 13×9-inch baking or roasting pan, shape into loaf. Top with remaining ½ cup pasta sauce.

3. Bake uncovered 50 minutes.

4. Sprinkle top with remaining ½ cup cheese. Bake an additional 10 minutes or until done. Let stand 10 minutes before serving.

Makes 8 servings

Recipe Tip: When grating cheese, spray your box grater with nonstick cooking spray and place on a sheet of waxed paper. When you finish grating, clean-up is a breeze. Simply discard the waxed paper and rinse the grater clean.

Pizza Meat Loaf

Zesty Italian Stuffed Peppers

   3 bell peppers (green, red or yellow)
   1 pound ground beef
   1 jar (14 ounces) spaghetti sauce
1⅓ cups *French's®* French Fried Onions, divided
   2 tablespoons *Frank's® RedHot®* Cayenne Pepper Sauce
  ½ cup uncooked instant rice
  ¼ cup sliced ripe olives
   1 cup (4 ounces) shredded mozzarella cheese

Preheat oven to 400°F. Cut bell peppers in half lengthwise through stems; discard seeds. Place pepper halves, cut side up, in 2-quart shallow baking dish; set aside.

Place beef in large microwavable bowl. Microwave on HIGH 5 minutes or until meat is browned, stirring once. Drain. Stir in spaghetti sauce, ⅔ *cup* French Fried Onions, **Frank's RedHot** Sauce, rice and olives. Spoon evenly into bell pepper halves.

Cover; bake 35 minutes or until bell peppers are tender. Uncover; sprinkle with cheese and remaining ⅔ *cup* onions. Bake 1 minute or until onions are golden. *Makes 6 servings*

Prep Time: 10 minutes
Cook Time: 36 minutes

Zesty Italian Stuffed Pepper

Beef Stroganoff Casserole

1 pound ground beef
¼ teaspoon salt
⅛ teaspoon black pepper
1 teaspoon vegetable oil
8 ounces sliced mushrooms
1 large onion, chopped
3 cloves garlic, minced
¼ cup dry white wine
1 can (10¾ ounces) condensed cream of mushroom soup, undiluted
½ cup sour cream
1 tablespoon Dijon mustard
4 cups cooked egg noodles
Chopped fresh parsley (optional)

1. Preheat oven to 350°F. Spray 13×9-inch baking dish with nonstick cooking spray.

2. Place beef in large skillet; season with salt and pepper. Brown beef over medium-high heat until no longer pink, stirring to separate beef. Drain fat from skillet; set beef aside.

3. Heat oil in same skillet over medium-high heat until hot. Add mushrooms, onion and garlic; cook and stir 2 minutes or until onion is tender. Add wine. Reduce heat to medium-low and simmer 3 minutes. Remove from heat; stir in soup, sour cream and mustard until well combined. Return beef to skillet.

4. Place noodles in prepared dish. Pour beef mixture over noodles; stir until noodles are well coated.

5. Bake, uncovered, 30 minutes or until heated through. Sprinkle with parsley, if desired. *Makes 6 servings*

Beef Stroganoff Casserole

Roasted Garlic Swedish Meatballs

   1 pound ground beef
½ cup plain dry bread crumbs
   1 egg
   1 jar (16 ounces) RAGÚ® Cheese Creations!® Roasted Garlic
      Parmesan Sauce
1¼ cups beef broth
   2 teaspoons Worcestershire sauce
   1 teaspoon ground allspice (optional)

In large bowl, combine ground beef, bread crumbs and egg; shape into 20 (1½-inch) meatballs.

In 12-inch nonstick skillet, brown meatballs over medium-high heat.

Meanwhile, in medium bowl, combine Ragú Cheese Creations! Sauce, beef broth, Worcestershire sauce and allspice; stir into skillet. Bring to a boil over high heat. Reduce heat to low and simmer uncovered, stirring occasionally, 10 minutes or until meatballs are done and sauce is slightly thickened. Serve, if desired, over hot cooked noodles or rice.

Makes 4 servings

Tip

Allspice, used in both sweet and savory dishes, tastes like a combination of cinnamon, nutmeg and cloves. Like other spices, it should be purchased in small amounts and stored in a cool, dark place for up to six months.

Roasted Garlic Swedish Meatballs

Souperior Meat Loaf

  2 pounds ground beef
  ¾ cup plain dry bread crumbs*
  1 envelope LIPTON® RECIPE SECRETS® Onion Soup Mix**
  ¾ cup water
  ⅓ cup ketchup
  2 eggs

Substitution: Use 1½ cups fresh bread crumbs or 5 slices fresh bread, cubed.

***Also terrific with LIPTON® RECIPE SECRETS® Beefy Onion, Onion Mushroom, Beefy Mushroom or Savory Herb with Garlic Soup Mix.*

1. Preheat oven to 350°F. In large bowl, combine all ingredients.

2. In 13×9-inch baking or roasting pan, shape into loaf.

3. Bake uncovered 1 hour or until done. Let stand 10 minutes before serving.   *Makes 8 servings*

Slow Cooker Method: Place meat loaf in slow cooker. Cover. Cook on HIGH 4 hours or LOW 6 to 8 hours.

Helpful Hint: Placing meat loaf on a piece of cheesecloth and then on a rack helps to hold the meat together while lifting in and out of slow cooker.

Recipe Tip: It's a snap to make fresh bread crumbs. Simply process fresh or day old white, Italian or French bread in a food processor or blender until fine crumbs form.

Prep Time: 10 minutes
Cook Time: 1 hour

Souperior Meat Loaf

Beefy Nacho Crescent Bake

    1 pound ground beef
    ½ cup chopped onion
    ¼ teaspoon salt
    ⅛ teaspoon black pepper
    1 tablespoon chili powder
    1 teaspoon ground cumin
    1 teaspoon dried oregano
    1 can (10¾ ounces) condensed nacho cheese soup, undiluted
    1 cup milk
    1 can (8 ounces) refrigerated crescent roll dough
    ¼ cup (1 ounce) shredded Cheddar cheese
      Chopped fresh cilantro (optional)

1. Preheat oven to 375°F. Spray 13×9-inch baking dish with nonstick cooking spray.

2. Place beef and onion in large skillet; season with salt and pepper. Brown beef 6 to 8 minutes over medium-high heat , stirring to separate meat. Drain fat. Stir in chili powder, cumin and oregano. Cook and stir 2 minutes; remove from heat.

3. Combine soup and milk in medium bowl, stirring until smooth. Pour soup mixture into prepared dish, spreading evenly.

4. Separate crescent dough into 4 rectangles; press perforations together firmly. Roll each rectangle to 8×4 inches. Cut each rectangle in half crosswise to form 8 (4-inch) squares.

5. Spoon about ¼ cup beef mixture in center of each square. Lift 4 corners of dough up over filling to meet in center; pinch and twist firmly to seal. Place squares in dish.

6. Bake, uncovered, 20 to 25 minutes or until crusts are golden brown. Sprinkle cheese over squares. Bake 5 minutes or until cheese melts. To serve, spoon soup mixture in dish over each serving; sprinkle with cilantro, if desired.   *Makes 4 servings*

Beefy Nacho Crescent Bake

Contadina® Classic Lasagne

1 pound dry lasagne noodles, cooked
1 tablespoon olive or vegetable oil
1 cup chopped onion
½ cup chopped green bell pepper
2 cloves garlic, minced
1½ pounds lean ground beef
2 cans (14.5 ounces each) CONTADINA® Recipe Ready Diced
    Tomatoes, undrained
1 can (8 ounces) CONTADINA® Tomato Sauce
1 can (6 ounces) CONTADINA® Tomato Paste
½ cup dry red wine or beef broth
1½ teaspoons salt
1 teaspoon dried oregano leaves, crushed
1 teaspoon dried basil leaves, crushed
½ teaspoon ground black pepper
1 egg
1 cup (8 ounces) ricotta cheese
2 cups (8 ounces) shredded mozzarella cheese, divided

1. Cook pasta according to package directions; drain. Meanwhile, heat oil in large skillet. Add onion, bell pepper and garlic; sauté for 3 minutes or until vegetables are tender. Add beef; cook for 5 to 6 minutes or until evenly browned.

2. Add tomatoes and juice, tomato sauce, tomato paste, wine, salt, oregano, basil and black pepper; bring to a boil. Reduce heat to low; simmer, uncovered, for 20 minutes, stirring occasionally.

3. Beat egg slightly in medium bowl. Stir in ricotta cheese and 1 cup mozzarella cheese.

4. Layer noodles, half of meat sauce, noodles, all of ricotta cheese mixture, noodles and remaining meat sauce in ungreased 13×9-inch baking dish. Sprinkle with remaining mozzarella cheese.

5. Bake in preheated 350°F oven for 25 to 30 minutes or until heated through. Let stand 10 minutes before cutting.   *Makes 10 servings*

Contadina® Classic Lasagne

Suzie's Sloppy Joes

3 pounds ground beef
1 cup chopped onion
3 cloves garlic, minced
1¼ cups ketchup
1 cup chopped red bell pepper
¼ cup plus 1 tablespoon Worcestershire sauce
¼ tablespoons brown sugar
3 tablespoons vinegar
3 tablespoons prepared mustard
2 teaspoons chili powder
Hamburger buns

SLOW COOKER DIRECTIONS

1. Brown beef, onion and garlic in large skillet 6 to 8 minutes over medium-high heat, stirring to break up meat. Drain fat.

2. Combine ketchup, bell pepper, Worcestershire sauce, brown sugar, vinegar, mustard and chili powder in slow cooker. Stir in beef mixture. Cover and cook on LOW 6 to 8 hours. Spoon into hamburger buns.

Makes 8 to 10 servings

Tip

There are many choices of ground beef in the supermarket; the names indicate the cut of meat that was ground. From the leanest to the fattest cut is ground sirloin, ground round and then ground chuck being the fattest.

Suzie's Sloppy Joes

Mexican Taco Salad

1 pound ground beef
1 cup (1 small) chopped onion
1 cup ORTEGA® Salsa Prima-Thick & Chunky Mild
¾ cup water
1 package (1¼ ounces) ORTEGA® Taco Seasoning Mix
1¾ cups (15-ounce can) kidney or pinto beans, rinsed and drained
½ cup (4-ounce can) ORTEGA® Diced Green Chiles
3 cups (3 ounces) tortilla chips or 6 tortilla shells
6 cups shredded lettuce, *divided*
Chopped tomatoes (optional)
¾ cup (3 ounces) shredded Nacho & Taco blend cheese, *divided*
Sour cream (optional)
Guacamole (optional)
ORTEGA® Thick & Smooth Taco Sauce

COOK beef and onion until beef is brown; drain. Stir in salsa, water and seasoning mix. Bring to a boil. Reduce heat to low; cook for 2 to 3 minutes. Stir in beans and chiles.

LAYER ingredients as follows on tortilla chips: *1 cup* lettuce, *¾ cup* meat mixture, tomatoes, *2 tablespoons* cheese and sour cream. Serve with guacamole and taco sauce. *Makes 6 servings*

Mexican Taco Salad

TRIED & TRUE
Casseroles

Layered Mexican Casserole

8 ounces ground beef
1 (12-ounce) can whole kernel corn, drained
1 (12-ounce) jar chunky salsa
1 (2¼-ounce) can sliced pitted ripe olives, drained
1 cup cream-style cottage cheese
1 (8-ounce) carton dairy sour cream
5 cups tortilla chips (7 to 8 ounces)
2 cups (8 ounces) shredded Wisconsin Cheddar cheese, divided
½ cup chopped tomato

Brown ground beef in large skillet; drain. Add corn and salsa; cook until thoroughly heated. Reserve 2 tablespoons olives; stir remaining olives into beef mixture. Combine cottage cheese and sour cream in bowl.

In 2-quart casserole, layer 2 cups chips, half of meat mixture, ¾ cup Cheddar cheese and half of cottage cheese mixture. Repeat layers; cover. Bake in preheated 350°F oven 35 minutes. Line edge of casserole with remaining 1 cup chips; top with tomato, reserved 2 tablespoons olives and remaining ½ cup Cheddar cheese. Bake 10 minutes or until cheese is melted. *Makes 4 to 6 servings*

*Favorite recipe from **Wisconsin Milk Marketing Board***

Shepherd's Pie

1⅓ cups instant mashed potatoes
1⅔ cups milk
  2 tablespoons butter or margarine
  1 teaspoon salt, divided
  1 pound ground beef
 ¼ teaspoon black pepper
  1 jar (12 ounces) beef gravy
  1 package (10 ounces) frozen mixed vegetables, thawed and
     drained
 ¾ cup grated Parmesan cheese

1. Preheat broiler. Prepare 4 servings of mashed potatoes according to package directions using milk, margarine and ½ teaspoon salt.

2. Meanwhile, brown meat in medium broilerproof skillet over medium-high heat, stirring to separate meat. Drain fat. Sprinkle meat with remaining ½ teaspoon salt and pepper. Add gravy and vegetables; mix well. Cook over medium-low heat 5 minutes or until hot.

3. Spoon prepared potatoes around outside edge of skillet, leaving 3-inch circle in center. Sprinkle cheese evenly over potatoes. Broil 4 to 5 inches from heat source 3 minutes or until cheese is golden brown and meat mixture is bubbly. *Makes 4 servings*

Prep and Cook Time: 28 minutes

Shepherd's Pie

Tamale Beef Squares

1 (6½-ounce) package corn muffin and corn bread mix
⅓ cup milk
¼ cup egg substitute
1 tablespoon canola oil
1 pound ground beef
¾ cup chopped onion
1 cup frozen corn kernels
1 (14½-ounce) can Mexican-style stewed tomatoes, undrained
2 teaspoons cornstarch
¾ cup shredded sharp Cheddar cheese (3 ounces)

1. Preheat oven to 400°F. Spray 12×8-inch baking dish with nonstick cooking spray.

2. Stir together corn muffin mix, milk, egg substitute and oil. Spread in bottom of prepared dish.

3. Brown beef and onion in large skillet 6 to 8 minutes over medium-high heat, stirring to break up meat. Drain fat. Stir in corn.

4. Mix together undrained tomatoes and cornstarch, breaking up any large pieces of tomato. Stir into beef mixture. Bring to a boil, stirring frequently.

5. Spoon beef mixture over corn bread mixture. Cover with foil. Bake 15 minutes. Uncover; bake 10 minutes more. Sprinkle with cheese. Return to oven; bake 2 to 3 minutes or until cheese melts. Let stand 5 minutes. Cut into squares. *Makes 6 servings*

Tamale Beef Squares

Artichoke Casserole

¾ **pound ground beef**
½ **cup sliced mushrooms**
¼ **cup chopped onion**
1 **clove garlic, minced**
1 **can (14 ounces) artichoke hearts, drained, rinsed and chopped**
½ **cup dry bread crumbs**
¼ **cup grated Parmesan cheese**
2 **tablespoons chopped fresh rosemary** *or* **1 teaspoon dried rosemary**
1½ **teaspoons chopped fresh marjoram** *or* ½ **teaspoon dried marjoram**
   Salt and black pepper
3 **egg whites**

1. Preheat oven to 400°F. Spray 1-quart casserole with nonstick cooking spray.

2. Brown beef in medium skillet 6 to 8 minutes over medium-high heat, stirring to break up meat. Drain fat. Add mushrooms, onion and garlic; cook until tender.

3. Combine ground beef mixture, artichokes, crumbs, cheese, rosemary and marjoram; mix lightly. Season with salt and pepper to taste.

4. Beat egg whites until stiff peaks form; fold into ground beef mixture. Spoon into prepared casserole.

5. Bake 20 minutes or until lightly browned around edges.

Makes 4 servings

Tortellini Bake Parmesano

1 package (12 ounces) fresh or frozen cheese tortellini or ravioli
½ pound lean ground beef
½ medium onion, finely chopped
2 cloves garlic, minced
½ teaspoon dried oregano, crushed
**1 can (26 ounces) DEL MONTE® Chunky Spaghetti Sauce with
    Garlic & Herb**
2 small zucchini, sliced
⅓ cup (about 1½ ounces) grated Parmesan cheese

1. Cook pasta according to package directions; rinse and drain.

2. Meanwhile, brown beef with onion, garlic and oregano in large skillet over medium-high heat; drain. Season with salt and pepper, if desired.

3. Add spaghetti sauce and zucchini. Cook 15 minutes or until thickened, stirring occasionally.

4. Arrange half of pasta in oiled 2-quart microwavable dish; top with half each of sauce and cheese. Repeat layers ending with cheese; cover.

5. Microwave on HIGH 8 to 10 minutes or until heated through, rotating dish halfway through cooking time.   *Makes 4 servings*

Hint: For convenience, double recipe and freeze one half for later use. The recipe can also be made ahead, refrigerated and heated just before serving (allow extra time in microwave if dish is chilled).

Prep and Cook Time: 35 minutes

Italian-Style Meat Loaf

1 egg
1½ pounds lean ground beef
8 ounces hot or mild Italian sausage, casings removed
1 cup CONTADINA® Seasoned Bread Crumbs
1 can (8 ounces) CONTADINA Tomato Sauce, divided
1 cup finely chopped onion
½ cup finely chopped green bell pepper

1. Beat egg lightly in large bowl. Add beef, sausage, bread crumbs, ¾ cup tomato sauce, onion and bell pepper; mix well.

2. Press into ungreased 9×5-inch loaf pan. Bake, uncovered, in preheated 350°F oven for 60 minutes.

3. Spoon remaining tomato sauce over meat loaf. Bake 15 minutes longer or until no longer pink in center; drain. Let stand for 10 minutes before serving. *Makes 8 servings*

Prep Time: 10 minutes
Cook Time: 75 minutes
Stand Time: 10 minutes

Italian-Style Meat Loaf

Moussaka

  1 large eggplant, cut lengthwise into ½-inch-thick slices
2½ teaspoons salt, divided
  ½ cup olive oil, divided
  2 russet potatoes, peeled, cut lengthwise into ¼-inch-thick slices
  2 large zucchini, cut lengthwise into ⅜-inch-thick slices
1½ pounds ground beef
  1 large onion, chopped
  2 cloves garlic, minced
  1 cup chopped tomatoes
  ½ cup dry red or white wine
  ¼ cup chopped fresh parsley
  ⅛ teaspoon *each* ground cinnamon and black pepper
  1 cup grated Parmesan cheese, divided
  4 tablespoons butter or margarine, divided
  ⅓ cup all-purpose flour
  ¼ teaspoon ground nutmeg
  2 cups milk

1. Place eggplant in colander; sprinkle with 1 teaspoon salt. Drain 30 minutes. Heat ¼ cup oil in skillet over medium heat. Add potatoes in single layer. Cook 5 minutes per side; drain. Add more oil to skillet; cook zucchini 2 minutes per side. Drain. Add more oil to skillet. Cook eggplant 5 minutes per side. Drain and discard oil.

2. Brown beef, onion and garlic in skillet 6 to 8 minutes over medium-high heat, stirring to break up meat. Drain fat. Stir in tomatoes, wine, parsley, 1 teaspoon salt, cinnamon and pepper. Bring to a boil. Reduce heat to low; simmer 10 minutes or until liquid evaporates.

3. Preheat oven to 325°F. Grease 13×9-inch baking dish. Layer potatoes, ¼ cup cheese, zucchini, ¼ cup cheese, eggplant and ¼ cup cheese and meat mixture. Melt butter in saucepan over low heat. Whisk in flour, remaining ½ teaspoon salt and nutmeg. Cook 1 minute; gradually add milk. Whisk over medium heat until mixture boils and thickens. Pour butter mixture over meat; sprinkle with remaining ¼ cup cheese. Bake 30 to 40 minutes.   *Makes 6 to 8 servings*

Quick Tamale Casserole

1½ **pounds ground beef**
¾ **cup sliced green onions**
  1 **can (4 ounces) chopped green chiles, drained and divided**
  1 **can (10¾ ounces) condensed tomato soup**
¾ **cup salsa**
  1 **can (16 ounces) whole kernel corn, drained**
  1 **can (2¼ ounces) chopped pitted ripe olives (optional)**
  1 **tablespoon Worcestershire sauce**
  1 **teaspoon chili powder**
¼ **teaspoon garlic powder**
  4 **slices (¾ ounce each) American cheese, halved**
  4 **corn muffins, cut into ½-inch cubes**
    Mexican Sour Cream Topping (recipe follows)

1. Brown beef and green onions 6 to 8 minutes over medium-high heat, stirring to break up meat. Drain fat. Reserve 2 tablespoons chiles for Mexican Sour Cream Topping. Stir in remaining chiles, tomato soup, salsa, corn, olives, Worcestershire sauce, chili powder and garlic powder until well blended.

2. Place mixture in 2-quart casserole. Top with cheese; spread muffin cubes over cheese. Prepare Mexican Sour Cream Topping. Bake at 350°F for 5 to 10 minutes or until cheese is melted. Top with Mexican Sour Cream Topping. *Makes 6 servings*

Mexican Sour Cream Topping: Mix 1 cup sour cream, 2 tablespoons chopped green chiles (reserved from above) and 2 teaspoons lime juice in small bowl until well blended. Makes about 1 cup.

Main-Dish Pie

1 package (8 rolls) refrigerated crescent rolls
1 pound lean ground beef
1 medium onion, chopped
1 can (12 ounces) beef or mushroom gravy
1 box (10 ounces) BIRDS EYE® frozen Green Peas, thawed
½ cup shredded Swiss cheese
6 slices tomato

• Preheat oven to 350°F.

• Unroll dough and separate rolls. Spread to cover bottom of ungreased 9-inch pie pan. Press together to form lower crust. Bake 10 minutes.

• Meanwhile, in large skillet, brown beef and onion; drain excess fat.

• Stir in gravy and peas; cook until heated through.

• Pour mixture into partially baked crust. Sprinkle with cheese.

• Bake 10 to 15 minutes or until crust is brown and cheese is melted.

• Arrange tomato slices over pie; bake 2 minutes more.

Makes 6 servings

Prep Time: 10 minutes
Cook Time: 20 to 25 minutes

Main-Dish Pie

Spaghetti Rolls

1 package (8 ounces) manicotti shells
2 pounds ground beef
1 tablespoon onion powder
1 teaspoon salt
½ teaspoon black pepper
2 cups spaghetti sauce, divided
1 cup (4 ounces) shredded mozzarella cheese or pizza-flavored
    cheese blend

1. Cook pasta according to package directions. Place in colander, then rinse under warm running water. Drain well.

2. Meanwhile, preheat oven to 350°F. Grease 13×9-inch baking pan.

3. Brown beef in large skillet 6 to 8 minutes over medium-high heat, stirring to break up meat. Drain fat. Stir in onion powder, salt and pepper. Stir in 1 cup spaghetti sauce; cool and set aside.

4. Reserve ½ cup ground beef mixture. Combine remaining beef mixture with cheese in large bowl. Fill shells with remaining beef mixture using spoon.

5. Arrange shells in prepared pan. Combine remaining 1 cup spaghetti sauce with reserved beef mixture in small bowl; blend well. Pour over shells. Cover with foil.

6. Bake 20 to 30 minutes or until hot. Garnish as desired.

Makes 4 servings

Chipotle Tamale Pie

¾ **pound ground beef**
1 **cup chopped onion**
¾ **cup diced green bell pepper**
¾ **cup diced red bell pepper**
4 **cloves garlic, minced**
2 **teaspoons ground cumin**
1 **can (15 ounces) pinto or red beans, rinsed and drained**
1 **can (8 ounces) no-salt-added stewed tomatoes, undrained**
2 **canned chipotle peppers in adobo sauce, minced**
    (about 1 tablespoon)
1 **to 2 teaspoons adobo sauce from canned peppers (optional)**
1 **cup (4 ounces) shredded Cheddar cheese**
½ **cup chopped fresh cilantro**
1 **package (8½ ounces) corn bread mix**
⅓ **cup milk**
1 **large egg white**

1. Preheat oven to 400°F. Spray 8-inch square baking dish with nonstick cooking spray.

2. Cook beef, onion, bell peppers and garlic in large nonstick skillet over medium-high heat 8 minutes or until beef is no longer pink, stirring occasionally. Drain fat. Sprinkle mixture with cumin.

3. Add beans, tomatoes, chipotle peppers and adobo sauce, if desired. Bring to a boil over high heat. Reduce heat to medium; simmer, uncovered, 5 minutes. Remove from heat; stir in cheese and cilantro.

4. Spoon beef mixture evenly into prepared dish, pressing down to compact mixture. Combine corn bread mix, milk and egg white in medium bowl; mix just until dry ingredients are moistened. Spoon batter evenly over beef mixture to cover completely.

5. Bake 20 to 22 minutes or until corn bread is golden brown. Let stand 5 minutes before serving. *Makes 6 servings*

Tried & True Casseroles

Hearty Lasagna Rolls

1½ pounds ground beef
  1 cup chopped fresh mushrooms
  1 medium onion, finely chopped
  1 small carrot, finely chopped
  1 clove garlic, finely chopped
  ¼ cup dry red wine or beef broth
  ⅛ teaspoon cayenne pepper (optional)
  2 cups shredded mozzarella cheese
  1 egg, slightly beaten
  5 tablespoons grated Parmesan cheese, divided
  1 jar (1 pound 10 ounces) RAGÚ® Robusto! Pasta Sauce
12 ounces lasagna noodles, cooked and drained

Preheat oven to 350°F. In 12-inch skillet, brown ground beef over medium-high heat; drain. Stir in mushrooms, onion, carrot and garlic and cook over medium heat, stirring occasionally, until vegetables are tender. Stir in wine and cayenne pepper; cook over high heat 3 minutes. Remove from heat; let stand 10 minutes.

In medium bowl, thoroughly combine ground beef mixture, mozzarella cheese, egg and 2 tablespoons Parmesan cheese. In 13×9-inch baking dish, evenly pour 2 cups Ragú Robusto! Pasta Sauce. Evenly spread ⅓ cup ground beef filling over each lasagna noodle. Carefully roll up noodles. Place seam-side-down in baking dish. Evenly spread remaining sauce over lasagna rolls. Bake covered 40 minutes. Sprinkle with remaining 3 tablespoons Parmesan cheese and bake uncovered 5 minutes or until bubbly. *Makes 6 servings*

Hearty Lasagna Rolls

Fiesta Beef Enchiladas

    8 ounces ground beef
   ½ cup sliced green onions
    2 teaspoons fresh minced garlic
    1 cup cooked rice
1½ cups chopped tomato, divided
   ¾ cup frozen corn, thawed
    1 cup (4 ounces) shredded Mexican cheese blend or Cheddar
       cheese, divided
   ½ cup salsa or picante sauce
  12 (6- to 7-inch) corn tortillas
      Nonstick cooking spray
    1 can (10 ounces) mild or hot enchilada sauce
    1 cup sliced romaine lettuce leaves

1. Preheat oven to 375°F. Brown beef in medium nonstick skillet 6 to 8 minutes over medium-high heat, stirring to break up meat. Drain fat. Add green onions and garlic; cook and stir 2 minutes.

2. Combine meat mixture, rice, 1 cup tomato, corn, ½ cup cheese and salsa; mix well. Spoon mixture down center of tortillas. Roll up; place seam side down in 13×9-inch baking dish that has been sprayed with cooking spray. Spoon enchilada sauce evenly over filled tortillas.

3. Cover with foil; bake 20 minutes or until hot. Sprinkle with remaining ½ cup cheese; bake 5 minutes or until cheese melts. Top with lettuce and remaining ½ cup tomato. *Makes 4 servings*

Prep Time: 15 minutes
Cook Time: 35 minutes

Pizza Pie Meatloaf

  2 pounds ground beef
1½ cups shredded mozzarella cheese, divided
  ½ cup unseasoned dry bread crumbs
  1 cup tomato sauce, divided
  ¼ cup grated Parmesan cheese
  ¼ cup *French's*® Worcestershire Sauce
  1 tablespoon dried oregano leaves
1⅓ cups *French's*® French Fried Onions

1. Preheat oven to 350°F. Combine beef, *½ cup* mozzarella, bread crumbs, *½ cup* tomato sauce, Parmesan cheese, Worcestershire and oregano in large bowl; stir with fork until well blended.

2. Place meat mixture into round pizza pan with edge or pie plate; shape into 9×1-inch round. Bake 35 minutes or until no longer pink in center and internal temperature reads 160°F. Drain fat.

3. Top with remaining tomato sauce, mozzarella cheese and French Fried Onions. Bake 5 minutes or until cheese is melted and onions are golden. Cut into wedges to serve.   *Makes 6 to 8 servings*

Prep Time: 10 minutes
Cook Time: 40 minutes

Tacos in Pasta Shells

1 package (3 ounces) cream cheese with chives
18 jumbo pasta shells
1¼ pounds ground beef
1 teaspoon salt
1 teaspoon chili powder
2 tablespoons butter, melted
1 cup prepared taco sauce
1 cup (4 ounces) shredded Cheddar cheese
1 cup (4 ounces) shredded Monterey Jack cheese
1½ cups crushed tortilla chips
1 cup sour cream
3 green onions, chopped
Leaf lettuce, small pitted ripe olives and cherry tomatoes (optional)

1. Cut cream cheese into ½-inch cubes. Let stand at room temperature until softened. Cook pasta according to package directions. Place in colander and rinse under warm running water. Drain well. Return to saucepan.

2. Meanwhile, preheat oven to 350°F. Butter 13×9-inch baking pan.

3. Brown beef in large skillet 6 to 8 minutes over medium-high heat, stirring to break up meat. Drain fat. Reduce heat to medium-low. Add cream cheese, salt and chili powder; simmer 5 minutes.

4. Toss shells with butter. Fill shells with beef mixture using spoon. Arrange shells in prepared pan. Pour taco sauce over each shell. Cover with foil.

5. Bake 15 minutes. Uncover; top with Cheddar cheese, Monterey Jack cheese and chips. Bake 15 minutes more or until bubbly. Top with sour cream and onions. Garnish with lettuce, olives and tomatoes.

Makes 4 to 6 servings

Tacos in Pasta Shells

Tamale Pie

1 tablespoon olive or vegetable oil
1 small onion, chopped
1 pound ground beef
1 envelope LIPTON® RECIPE SECRETS® Onion Soup Mix*
1 can (14½ ounces) stewed tomatoes, undrained
½ cup water
1 can (15 to 19 ounces) red kidney beans, rinsed and drained
1 package (8½ ounces) corn muffin mix

Also terrific with LIPTON® RECIPE SECRETS® Fiesta Herb with Red Pepper, Onion-Mushroom, Beefy Onion or Beefy Mushroom Soup Mix.

• Preheat oven to 400°F.

• In 12-inch skillet, heat oil over medium heat and cook onion, stirring occasionally, 3 minutes or until tender. Stir in ground beef and cook until browned.

• Stir in onion soup mix blended with tomatoes and water. Bring to a boil over high heat, stirring with spoon to crush tomatoes. Reduce heat to low and stir in beans. Simmer uncovered, stirring occasionally, 10 minutes. Turn into 2-quart casserole.

• Prepare corn muffin mix according to package directions. Spoon evenly over casserole.

• Bake uncovered 15 minutes or until corn topping is golden and filling is hot.   *Makes about 6 servings*

Cheddar Burger Mashed Potato Bake

2 pounds ground beef
1 medium onion, chopped
1 jar (16 ounces) RAGÚ® Cheese Creations!® Double Cheddar Sauce
2 teaspoons dry mustard
4 cups prepared mashed potatoes

Preheat oven to 425°F. In 12-inch skillet, brown ground beef over medium-high heat; drain. Add onion and cook, stirring occasionally, 2 minutes. Stir in Ragú Cheese Creations! Sauce, mustard and, if desired, salt and ground black pepper to taste. Simmer uncovered, stirring occasionally, 3 minutes or until heated through.

Turn into 2-quart casserole; evenly top with mashed potatoes. Bake uncovered 25 minutes or until potatoes are lightly golden.

Makes 8 servings

Recipe Tip: When making mashed potatoes, use Idaho or all-purpose potatoes for marvelous flavor and texture. Heat the milk before adding it—this minimizes any starchiness.

Chili Spaghetti Casserole

8 ounces uncooked spaghetti
1 pound ground beef
1 medium onion, chopped
¼ teaspoon salt
⅛ teaspoon black pepper
1 can (15 ounces) vegetarian chili with beans
1 can (14½ ounces) Italian-style stewed tomatoes, undrained
1½ cups (6 ounces) shredded sharp Cheddar cheese, divided
½ cup sour cream
1½ teaspoons chili powder
¼ teaspoon garlic powder

1. Preheat oven to 350°F. Spray 13×9-inch baking dish with nonstick cooking spray.

2. Cook pasta according to package directions. Drain and place in prepared dish.

3. Meanwhile, place beef and onion in large skillet; season with salt and pepper. Brown beef 6 to 8 minutes over medium-high heat, stirring to break up meat. Drain fat. Stir in chili, tomatoes with juice, 1 cup cheese, sour cream, chili powder and garlic powder.

4. Add chili mixture to pasta; stir until pasta is well coated. Sprinkle with remaining ½ cup cheese.

5. Cover tightly with foil and bake 30 minutes or until hot and bubbly. Let stand 5 minutes before serving.   *Makes 8 servings*

Chili Spaghetti Casserole

Patchwork Casserole

2 pounds ground beef
2 cups chopped green bell pepper
1 cup chopped onion
2 pounds frozen Southern-style hash brown potatoes, thawed
2 cans (8 ounces each) tomato sauce
1 cup water
1 can (6 ounces) tomato paste
1 teaspoon salt
½ teaspoon dried basil, crumbled
¼ teaspoon black pepper
1 pound pasteurized process American cheese, thinly sliced

1. Preheat oven to 350°F.

2. Brown beef 6 to 8 minutes in large skillet over medium-high heat, stirring to break up meat. Drain fat.

3. Add bell pepper and onion; cook and stir until tender, about 4 minutes. Stir in potatoes, tomato sauce, water, tomato paste, salt, basil and black pepper.

4. Spoon half of mixture into 13×9-inch baking pan or 3-quart baking dish; top with half of cheese. Spoon remaining meat mixture evenly on top of cheese. Cover pan with aluminum foil. Bake 45 minutes.

5. Cut remaining cheese into decorative shapes; place on top of casserole. Let stand loosely covered until cheese melts, about 5 minutes.

Makes 8 to 10 servings

Silly Spaghetti Casserole

8 ounces uncooked spaghetti
¼ cup cholesterol-free egg substitute
¼ cup finely shredded Parmesan cheese
½ (10-ounce) package frozen cut spinach, thawed
¾ pound ground beef
⅓ cup chopped onion
2 cups prepared spaghetti sauce
¾ cup shredded part-skim mozzarella cheese (3 ounces)
1 green or yellow bell pepper

1. Preheat oven to 350°F. Spray 8-inch square baking dish with nonstick cooking spray.

2. Cook spaghetti according to package directions; drain. Toss with egg substitute and Parmesan cheese. Place in bottom of prepared baking dish.

3. Drain spinach in colander, pressing out excess liquid. Spray large nonstick skillet with cooking spray. Cook beef and onion in skillet over medium-high heat until meat is lightly browned, stirring to break up meat. Drain fat. Stir in spinach and spaghetti sauce. Spoon on top of spaghetti mixture.

4. Sprinkle with mozzarella cheese. Use small cookie cutter to cut decorative shapes from bell pepper. Place on top of cheese in baking dish. Cover dish with foil. Bake 40 to 45 minutes or until bubbly. Let stand 10 minutes. Cut into squares. *Makes 6 servings*

Tried & True Casseroles

Simple
SKILLET DISHES

Italian Beef Burritos

1½ pounds ground beef
2 medium onions, finely chopped
2 medium red and/or green bell peppers, chopped
1 jar (26 to 28 ounces) RAGÚ® Robusto!™ Pasta Sauce
½ teaspoon dried oregano leaves, crushed
8 (10-inch) flour tortillas, warmed
2 cups shredded mozzarella cheese (about 8 ounces)

1. In 12-inch skillet, brown ground beef over medium-high heat.

2. Stir in onions and red bell peppers and cook, stirring occasionally, 5 minutes or until tender; drain. Stir in Ragú Pasta Sauce and oregano; heat through.

3. To serve, top each tortilla with ¼ cup cheese and 1 cup ground beef mixture; roll up and serve.

Makes 8 servings

Prep Time: 15 minutes
Cook Time: 15 minutes

Malaysian Curried Beef

2 tablespoons vegetable oil
2 large yellow onions, chopped
1 piece fresh ginger (about 1-inch square), minced
2 cloves garlic, minced
2 tablespoons curry powder
1 teaspoon salt
2 large baking potatoes (1 pound), peeled and cut into chunks
1 cup beef broth
1 pound ground beef
2 ripe tomatoes (12 ounces), peeled and cut into chunks
  Hot cooked rice

1. Heat wok over medium-high heat 1 minute or until hot. Drizzle oil into wok and heat 30 seconds. Add onions and stir-fry 2 minutes. Add ginger, garlic, curry and salt; cook and stir about 1 minute or until fragrant. Add potatoes; cook and stir 2 to 3 minutes.

2. Add beef broth to potato mixture. Cover and bring to a boil. Reduce heat to low; simmer about 20 minutes or until potatoes are fork-tender.

3. Stir ground beef into potato mixture. Cook and stir about 5 minutes or until beef is browned and no pink remains; spoon off fat.

4. Add tomato chunks and stir gently until thoroughly heated. Spoon beef mixture into serving dish. Top center with rice.

Makes 4 servings

Malaysian Curried Beef

Ragú® Chili Mac

1 tablespoon olive or vegetable oil
1 medium green bell pepper, chopped
1 pound ground beef
1 jar (26 to 28 ounces) RAGÚ® Old World Style® Pasta Sauce
2 tablespoons chili powder
8 ounces elbow macaroni, cooked and drained

1. In 12-inch nonstick skillet, heat oil over medium-high heat and cook bell pepper, stirring occasionally, 3 minutes. Add ground beef and brown, stirring occasionally; drain.

2. Stir in Ragú Pasta Sauce and chili powder. Bring to a boil over high heat. Reduce heat to low and simmer covered 10 minutes.

3. Stir in macaroni and heat through. Serve, if desired, with sour cream and shredded Cheddar cheese.   *Makes 4 servings*

Prep Time: 10 minutes
Cook Time: 25 minutes

Store ground beef in the coldest part of the refrigerator for up to 2 days, or wrap in plastic wrap and place in airtight container. Freeze for up to 3 months.

Ragú® Chili Mac

Onion Sloppy Joes

    1½ **pounds ground beef**
     1 **envelope LIPTON® RECIPE SECRETS® Onion Soup Mix**
     1 **cup water**
     1 **cup ketchup**
     2 **tablespoons firmly packed brown sugar**

In 10-inch skillet, brown ground beef over medium-high heat; drain.

Stir in remaining ingredients. Bring to a boil over high heat.

Reduce heat to low and simmer uncovered, stirring occasionally, 8 minutes or until mixture thickens. Serve, if desired, on hoagie rolls or hamburger buns. *Makes about 6 servings*

Menu Suggestion: Serve with a lettuce and tomato salad, tortilla chips and ice cream with a choice of toppings.

Greek Beef & Rice

    1 **bag SUCCESS® Rice**
    1 **pound lean ground beef**
    2 **medium zucchini, sliced**
    ½ **cup chopped onion**
    1 **medium clove garlic, minced**
    1 **can (14½ ounces) tomato sauce**
    ¾ **teaspoon dried basil leaves, crushed**
    ¾ **teaspoon salt**
    ¼ **teaspoon pepper**

Prepare rice according to package directions.

Brown beef in large skillet, stirring occasionally to separate beef. Pour off all but 2 tablespoons drippings. Add zucchini, onion and garlic to skillet; cook and stir until crisp-tender. Add all remaining ingredients *except* rice; cover. Simmer 10 minutes, stirring occasionally. Add rice; heat thoroughly, stirring occasionally. Garnish, if desired.
Makes about 6 servings

Szechwan Beef

1 pound ground beef
1 tablespoon vegetable oil
1 cup sliced carrots
1 cup frozen peas
⅓ cup water
3 tablespoons soy sauce
2 tablespoons cornstarch
¼ teaspoon ground ginger
1 jar (7 ounces) baby corn
1 medium onion, thinly sliced
   Sliced mushrooms and olives as desired
¼ cup shredded Cheddar Cheese
1⅓ cups uncooked instant rice

1. In wok or large skillet, brown ground beef; remove from wok and set aside. Drain fat.

2. Add oil to wok and return to medium heat. Add carrots and peas and stir-fry about 3 minutes.

3. In small cup blend water, soy sauce, cornstarch and ginger. Add to vegetables in wok.

4. Return ground beef to wok along with baby corn, onion, mushrooms, olives and cheese. Cook over medium heat until all ingredients are heated through.

5. Prepare instant rice according to package directions. Serve beef and vegetables over rice.   *Makes 4 to 5 servings*

*Favorite recipe from **North Dakota Beef Commission***

Broccoli and Beef Pasta

1 pound ground beef
2 cloves garlic, minced
1 can (about 14 ounces) beef broth
1 medium onion, thinly sliced
1 cup uncooked rotini pasta
½ teaspoon dried basil
½ teaspoon dried oregano
½ teaspoon dried thyme
1 can (15 ounces) Italian-style tomatoes, undrained
2 cups broccoli florets *or* 1 package (10 ounces) frozen broccoli, thawed
¾ cup (3 ounces) shredded Cheddar cheese or grated Parmesan cheese

1. Brown beef in large nonstick skillet 6 to 8 minutes over medium-high heat, stirring to break up meat. Drain fat. Transfer to large bowl; set aside.

2. Add broth, onion, pasta, basil, oregano and thyme to skillet. Bring to a boil. Reduce heat to medium-high and boil 10 minutes; add tomatoes with juice. Increase heat to high and bring to a boil; stir in broccoli. Cook, uncovered, 6 to 8 minutes, stirring occasionally, until broccoli is crisp-tender and pasta is tender (if using frozen broccoli, boil 15 minutes). Return meat to skillet and stir 3 to 4 minutes or until heated through.

3. Transfer to serving platter with slotted spoon. Sprinkle with cheese. Cover with lid several minutes, until cheese melts. Meanwhile, bring liquid left in skillet to a boil over high heat. Boil until thick and reduced to 3 to 4 tablespoons. Spoon over pasta.

Makes 4 servings

Serving Suggestion: Serve with garlic bread.

Prep and Cook Time: 30 minutes

Broccoli and Beef Pasta

Simple Skillet Dishes

Skillet Spaghetti and Sausage

¼ **pound mild or hot Italian sausage links, sliced**
½ **pound ground beef**
¼ **teaspoon dried oregano, crushed**
 4 **ounces spaghetti, broken in half**
 1 **can (14½ ounces) DEL MONTE® Diced Tomatoes with Basil,**
    Garlic & Oregano
 1 **can (8 ounces) DEL MONTE® Tomato Sauce**
1½ **cups sliced fresh mushrooms**
 2 **stalks celery, sliced**

1. Brown sausage in large skillet over medium-high heat. Add beef and oregano; season to taste with salt and pepper, if desired.

2. Cook, stirring occasionally, until beef is browned; drain.

3. Add pasta, 1 cup water, undrained tomatoes, tomato sauce, mushrooms and celery. Bring to boil, stirring occasionally.

4. Reduce heat; cover and simmer 12 to 14 minutes or until spaghetti is tender. Garnish with grated Parmesan cheese and chopped parsley, if desired. Serve immediately. *Makes 4 to 6 servings*

Prep Time: 5 minutes
Cook Time: 30 minutes

Pasta Beef & Zucchini Dinner

1 pound extra-lean ground beef
1 medium onion, chopped
1 clove garlic, crushed
½ teaspoon salt
2 (14-ounce) cans ready-to-serve beef broth
1 teaspoon Italian seasoning
¼ teaspoon crushed red pepper
2 cups uncooked mini lasagna or rotini pasta
2 cups sliced zucchini (cut ⅜ inch thick)
1 tablespoon cornstarch
¼ cup water
3 plum tomatoes, each cut into 4 wedges
2 tablespoons grated Parmesan cheese

In large nonstick skillet, cook ground beef with onion, garlic and salt over medium heat 8 to 10 minutes or until beef is browned, stirring occasionally to break up beef into 1-inch crumbles. Remove beef mixture with slotted spoon; pour off drippings. Set aside.

Add broth, Italian seasoning and red pepper to same skillet. Bring to a boil; add pasta. Reduce heat to medium; simmer, uncovered, for 6 minutes, stirring occasionally. Add zucchini; continue cooking for an additional 6 to 8 minutes or until pasta is tender yet firm. Push pasta and zucchini to side of skillet. Mix cornstarch with water and add to broth in skillet; bring to a boil. Return beef mixture to skillet. Add tomatoes; heat through, stirring occasionally. Spoon into serving dish; sprinkle with Parmesan cheese. *Makes 5 servings*

Favorite recipe from **North Dakota Wheat Commission**

Curry Beef

12 ounces wide egg noodles *or* 1⅓ cups long-grain white rice
1 tablespoon olive oil
1 medium onion, thinly sliced
1 tablespoon curry powder
1 teaspoon ground cumin
2 cloves garlic, minced
1 pound ground beef
1 cup (8 ounces) sour cream
½ cup milk
½ cup raisins, divided
1 teaspoon sugar
¼ cup chopped walnuts, almonds or pecans

1. Cook noodles according to package directions. Meanwhile, heat oil in large skillet over medium-high heat until hot. Add onion; cook and stir 3 to 4 minutes. Add curry powder, cumin and garlic; cook 2 to 3 minutes longer or until onion is tender. Add meat; cook 6 to 8 minutes, stirring to break up meat. Drain fat.

2. Stir in sour cream, milk, ¼ cup raisins and sugar. Reduce heat to medium; cook, stirring constantly, until heated through. Spoon over hot noodles. Sprinkle with remaining ¼ cup raisins and nuts.

Makes 4 servings

Serving Suggestion: Serve with sliced cucumber sprinkled with sugar and vinegar or plain yogurt topped with brown sugar, chopped bananas and green onions.

Prep and Cook Time: 30 minutes

Quick Greek Pitas

1 pound ground beef
1 package (10 ounces) frozen chopped spinach, thawed and
    well drained
4 green onions, chopped
1 can (2¼ ounces) sliced black olives, drained
1 teaspoon dried oregano, divided
¼ teaspoon black pepper
1 large tomato, diced
1 cup plain yogurt
½ cup mayonnaise
6 (6-inch) pita breads, warmed
    Lettuce leaves
1 cup (4 ounces) crumbled feta cheese

1. Brown beef in large skillet 6 to 8 minutes over medium-high heat, stirring to break up meat. Drain fat. Add spinach, green onions, olives, ½ teaspoon oregano and pepper; cook and stir 2 minutes. Stir in tomato.

2. Combine yogurt, mayonnaise and remaining ½ teaspoon oregano in small bowl. Split open pita breads; line each with lettuce leaf. Stir cheese into beef mixture and divide among pita pockets. Serve with yogurt sauce. *Makes 6 servings*

Cheeseburger Macaroni

1 cup mostaccioli or elbow macaroni, uncooked
1 pound ground beef
1 medium onion, chopped
1 can (14½ ounces) DEL MONTE® Diced Tomatoes with Basil, Garlic
    & Oregano
¼ cup DEL MONTE® Tomato Ketchup
1 cup (4 ounces) shredded Cheddar cheese

1. Cook pasta according to package directions; drain.

2. Brown meat with onion in large skillet; drain. Season with salt and pepper, if desired. Stir in undrained tomatoes, ketchup and pasta; heat through.

3. Top with cheese. Garnish, if desired.   *Makes 4 servings*

Prep Time: 8 minutes
Cook Time: 15 minutes

Tip If you'll be cooking this dish often for your kids, cook twice the amount of pasta called for and reserve it for another meal. Drain the extra portion well and toss it with a teaspoon of oil. Cover and refrigerate for up to three days.

Cheeseburger Macaroni

Simple Skillet Dishes

Taco Pot Pie

  1 pound ground beef
  1 package (1.25 ounces) taco seasoning mix
¼ cup water
  1 can (8 ounces) kidney beans, rinsed and drained
  1 cup chopped tomato
¾ cup frozen corn, thawed
¾ cup frozen peas, thawed
1½ cups (6 ounces) shredded Cheddar cheese
  1 can (11½ ounces) refrigerated corn breadstick dough

1. Preheat oven to 400°F. Brown beef in medium ovenproof skillet 6 to 8 minutes, stirring to break up meat. Drain fat. Add seasoning mix and water to skillet. Cook over medium-low heat 3 minutes or until most of liquid is absorbed, stirring occasionally.

2. Stir in beans, tomato, corn and peas. Cook 3 minutes or until mixture is hot. Remove from heat; stir in cheese.

3. Unwrap corn bread dough; separate into 16 strips. Twist strips, cutting to fit skillet. Arrange attractively over meat mixture. Press ends of dough lightly to edge of skillet to secure. Bake 15 minutes or until corn bread is golden brown and meat mixture is bubbly.

Makes 4 to 6 servings

Prep and Cook Time: 30 minutes

Beef with Snow Peas & Baby Corn

¾ **pound ground beef**
1 **clove garlic, minced**
1 **teaspoon vegetable oil**
6 **ounces snow peas, halved lengthwise**
1 **red bell pepper, cut into strips**
1 **can (15 ounces) baby corn, drained and rinsed**
1 **tablespoon soy sauce**
1 **teaspoon sesame oil**
   Salt and black pepper
2 **cups cooked rice**

1. Brown beef in wok or large skillet 6 to 8 minutes over medium-high heat, stirring to break up meat. Drain fat. Add garlic; cook until tender. Transfer to medium bowl; set aside. Wipe out wok with paper towel.

2. Heat vegetable oil in wok over medium-high heat. Add snow peas and red bell pepper; stir-fry 2 to 3 minutes or until vegetables are crisp-tender. Stir in ground beef mixture, baby corn, soy sauce and sesame oil; cook until heated through. Season with salt and black pepper to taste. Serve over rice. *Makes 4 servings*

Tip

Baby corn is a popular ingredient in Asian cooking. It is available in cans or jars, and it is found in the canned vegetable or ethnic section of most supermarkets.

Soups,
STEWS & CHILIS

Rapid Ragú® Chili

1½ pounds lean ground beef
1 medium onion, chopped
2 tablespoons chili powder
1 can (19 ounces) red kidney beans, rinsed and drained
1 jar (26 to 28 ounces) RAGÚ® Old World Style® Pasta
Sauce
1 cup shredded Cheddar cheese (about 4 ounces)

1. In 12-inch skillet, brown ground beef with onion and chili powder over medium-high heat, stirring occasionally. Stir in beans and Ragú Pasta Sauce.

2. Bring to a boil over high heat. Reduce heat to low and simmer covered, stirring occasionally, 20 minutes. Top with cheese. Serve, if desired, over hot cooked rice.

Makes 6 servings

Prep Time: 10 minutes
Cook Time: 25 minutes

All-in-One Burger Stew

1 pound ground beef
2 cups frozen Italian vegetables
1 can (14½ ounces) chopped tomatoes with basil and garlic,
    undrained
1 can (about 14 ounces) beef broth
2½ cups uncooked medium egg noodles
    Salt and black pepper

1. Brown beef in Dutch oven or large skillet 6 to 8 minutes over medium-high heat, stirring to break up meat. Drain fat.

2. Add vegetables, tomatoes with juice and broth; bring to a boil over high heat.

3. Add noodles; reduce heat to medium. Cover and cook 12 to 15 minutes or until noodles have absorbed liquid and vegetables are tender. Add salt and pepper to taste.   *Makes 6 servings*

Note: For a special touch, sprinkle with chopped parsley before serving.

Tip: To complete this meal, serve with breadsticks or a loaf of Italian bread.

Prep and Cook Time: 25 minutes

Soups, Stews & Chilis

Chile con Carne

    2 tablespoons vegetable oil
    2 pounds ground beef
    2 cups (2 small) chopped onions
    4 cloves garlic, finely chopped
 3½ cups (two 15-ounce cans) kidney, pinto or black beans, drained
 3½ cups (29-ounce can) crushed tomatoes
 1¾ cups (16-ounce jar) ORTEGA® Salsa Prima-Thick & Chunky Mild
  ½ cup dry white wine
  ½ cup (4-ounce can) ORTEGA® Diced Green Chiles
    3 tablespoons chili powder
    1 to 2 tablespoons ORTEGA® Diced Jalapeños
    1 tablespoon ground cumin
    1 tablespoon dried oregano, crushed
    2 teaspoons salt

HEAT vegetable oil in large saucepan over medium-high heat. Add beef, onions and garlic; cook for 4 to 5 minutes or until beef is no longer pink; drain.

STIR in beans, crushed tomatoes, salsa, wine, chiles, chili powder, jalapeños, cumin, oregano and salt. Bring to a boil. Reduce heat to low; cover. Cook, stirring frequently, for 1 hour.

Makes 10 to 12 servings

Hamburger Soup

1 pound ground beef
1 envelope (1 ounce) dried onion soup mix
1 envelope (1 ounce) Italian seasoning mix
¼ teaspoon seasoned salt
¼ teaspoon black pepper
3 cups boiling water
1 can (8 ounces) diced tomatoes, undrained
1 can (8 ounces) tomato sauce
1 tablespoon soy sauce
1 cup sliced celery
1 cup thinly sliced carrots
2 cups cooked macaroni
¼ cup grated Parmesan cheese
2 tablespoons chopped fresh parsley

SLOW COOKER DIRECTIONS

1. Brown beef in medium skillet 6 to 8 minutes over medium-high heat, stirring to break up meat. Drain fat. Add beef to slow cooker. Add soup mix, Italian seasoning, seasoned salt and pepper. Stir in water, tomatoes with juice, tomato sauce and soy sauce. Add celery and carrots. Cover and cook on LOW 6 to 8 hours.

2. Increase heat to HIGH; stir in cooked macaroni and Parmesan cheese. Cover and cook 10 to 15 minutes. Sprinkle with parsley just before serving. *Makes 6 to 8 servings*

Hamburger Soup

Albóndigas Soup

  1 pound ground beef
¼ **cup long-grain rice**
  1 egg
  1 tablespoon chopped fresh cilantro
  1 teaspoon LAWRY'S® Seasoned Salt
¼ **cup ice water**
  2 cans (14½ ounces each) chicken broth
  1 can (14½ ounces) whole peeled tomatoes, undrained and cut up
  1 stalk celery, diced
  1 large carrot, diced
  1 medium potato, diced
¼ **cup chopped onion**
¼ **teaspoon LAWRY'S® Garlic Powder with Parsley**

In medium bowl, combine ground beef, rice, egg, cilantro, Seasoned Salt and ice water; mix well and form into small meatballs. In large saucepan, combine broth, tomatoes with juice, celery, carrot, potato, onion and Garlic Powder with Parsley. Bring to a boil over medium-high heat; add meatballs. Reduce heat to low; cover and cook 30 to 40 minutes, stirring occasionally. *Makes 6 to 8 servings*

Serving Suggestion: Serve with lemon wedges and warm tortillas.

92

Farmer's Stew Argentina

3 cups water
1 pound lean ground beef
2 tablespoons vegetable oil
1 medium onion, chopped
1 green bell pepper, cut into ½-inch pieces
1 red bell pepper, cut into ½-inch pieces
1 small sweet potato, peeled and cut into ½-inch pieces
1 large clove garlic, minced
1 tablespoon chopped fresh parsley
1 teaspoon salt
½ teaspoon granulated sugar
⅛ teaspoon ground cumin
3 cups beef broth, heated
½ pound zucchini, cut into ½-inch pieces
1 cup whole kernel corn
2 tablespoons raisins
1 teaspoon TABASCO® brand Pepper Sauce
1 small pear, firm but ripe, cut into 1-inch pieces
6 cups cooked white rice

Bring water to a boil in large saucepan. Remove saucepan from heat. Add ground beef, stirring to break meat into little pieces. Let stand 5 minutes, stirring once or twice, until most of the pink disappears from meat. Drain meat well, discarding water.

Heat oil in large deep skillet or Dutch oven over medium-high heat. Add onion and cook 4 to 5 minutes, stirring constantly, until limp and slightly brown. Add beef. Cook, stirring constantly, until all liquid has evaporated and meat is lightly browned, about 10 minutes.

Reduce heat to medium. Add bell peppers, sweet potato and garlic. Continue cooking and stirring 5 minutes, or until peppers and potatoes are slightly tender. Add parsley, salt, sugar and cumin. Stir and cook 1 minute to blend flavors. Pour beef broth into skillet. Add zucchini, corn, raisins and TABASCO® Sauce. Simmer gently 10 minutes, being careful not to boil. Add pear and simmer 10 additional minutes, or until all fruits and vegetables are tender. Ladle over rice in individual serving bowls. *Makes 6 servings*

Hungarian Goulash Stew

¾ **pound lean ground beef (80% lean)**
½ **cup chopped onion**
 1 **clove garlic, minced**
 1 **package (4.8 ounces) PASTA RONI® Angel Hair Pasta with Herbs**
 1 **can (14½ ounces) diced tomatoes, undrained**
 1 **cup frozen corn *or* 1 can (8 ounces) whole kernel corn, drained**
1½ **teaspoons paprika**
 ⅛ **teaspoon black pepper**
   Sour cream (optional)

1. In 3-quart saucepan, brown ground beef, onion and garlic; drain.

2. Add 1⅓ cups water, pasta, Special Seasonings, tomatoes, corn and seasonings. Bring just to a boil.

3. Reduce heat to medium.

4. Boil uncovered, stirring frequently, 5 to 6 minutes or until pasta is tender.

5. Let stand 3 minutes or until desired consistency. Stir before serving. Serve with sour cream, if desired.   *Makes 4 servings*

Beefy Broccoli & Cheese Soup

2 cups chicken broth
1 package (10 ounces) frozen chopped broccoli, thawed
¼ cup chopped onion
¼ pound ground beef
1 cup milk
2 tablespoons all-purpose flour
1 cup (4 ounces) shredded sharp Cheddar cheese
1½ teaspoons chopped fresh oregano *or* ½ teaspoon dried oregano
    Salt and black pepper
    Hot pepper sauce

1. Bring broth to a boil in medium saucepan. Add broccoli and onion; cook 5 minutes or until broccoli is tender.

2. Meanwhile, brown ground beef in small skillet 6 to 8 minutes over medium-high heat, stirring to break up meat. Drain fat. Gradually add milk to flour in small bowl, mixing until well blended. Add milk mixture with ground beef to broth mixture and cook, stirring constantly, until mixture is thickened and bubbly.

3. Add cheese and oregano; stir until cheese is melted. Season with salt, pepper and hot pepper sauce to taste.   *Makes 4 to 5 servings*

Texas Beef Stew

    1 pound lean ground beef
    1 small onion, chopped
    1 can (28 ounces) crushed tomatoes with roasted garlic
1½ cups BIRDS EYE® frozen Farm Fresh Mixtures Broccoli,
        Cauliflower & Carrots
    1 can (14½ ounces) whole new potatoes, halved
    1 cup BIRDS EYE® frozen Sweet Corn
    1 can (4½ ounces) chopped green chilies, drained
    ½ cup water

• In large saucepan, cook beef and onion over medium-high heat until beef is well browned, stirring occasionally.

• Stir in tomatoes, vegetables, potatoes with liquid, corn, chilies and water; bring to boil.

• Reduce heat to medium-low; cover and simmer 5 minutes or until heated through.   *Makes 4 servings*

Serving Suggestion: Serve over rice with warm crusty bread.

Tip: The smell of onions and garlic can penetrate into your cutting boards. Keep a separate cutting board exclusively for these vegetables.

Prep Time: 5 minutes
Cook Time: 15 minutes

Texas Beef Stew

Hearty Chili Mac

1 pound ground beef
1 can (14½ ounces) diced tomatoes, drained
1 cup chopped onion
1 clove garlic, minced
1 tablespoon chili powder
½ teaspoon salt
½ teaspoon ground cumin
½ teaspoon dried oregano
¼ teaspoon black pepper
¼ teaspoon red pepper flakes
2 cups cooked macaroni

SLOW COOKER DIRECTIONS

1. Crumble ground beef into slow cooker. Add remaining ingredients, except macaroni, to slow cooker.

2. Cover and cook on LOW 4 hours.

3. Stir in cooked macaroni. Cover and cook on LOW 1 hour.

Makes 4 servings

Tip

When preparing pasta to be used in a slow cooker, soup or casserole recipe, it's a good idea to reduce the cooking time by one third. The pasta will continue to cook and absorb liquid in the final dish.

Kansas City Steak Soup

½ **pound ground beef**
1 **cup chopped onion**
3 **cups frozen mixed vegetables**
2 **cups water**
1 **can (14½ ounces) stewed tomatoes, undrained**
1 **cup sliced celery**
1 **beef bouillon cube**
½ **to 1 teaspoon black pepper**
1 **can (10½ ounces) beef broth**
½ **cup all-purpose flour**

1. Spray Dutch oven with nonstick cooking spray. Heat over medium-high heat until hot. Add beef and onion. Brown beef 6 to 8 minutes, stirring to break up meat. Drain fat.

2. Add vegetables, water, tomatoes with juice, celery, bouillon cube and pepper. Bring to a boil. Whisk together beef broth and flour until smooth; add to beef mixture, stirring constantly. Return mixture to a boil. Reduce heat to low. Cover and simmer 15 minutes, stirring frequently.   *Makes 6 servings*

Note: If time permits, allow the soup to simmer an additional 30 minutes—the flavors just get better and better.

Spicy Quick and Easy Chili

1 pound ground beef
1 large clove garlic, minced
1 can (15¼ ounces) DEL MONTE® Whole Kernel Golden Sweet Corn,
   drained
1 can (16 ounces) kidney beans, drained
1½ cups salsa, mild, medium or hot
1 can (4 ounces) diced green chiles, undrained

1. Brown meat with garlic in large saucepan; drain.

2. Add remaining ingredients. Simmer, uncovered, 10 minutes, stirring occasionally. Sprinkle with chopped green onions, if desired.

Makes 4 servings

Cheeseburger Macaroni Stew

1 pound ground beef
1 can (28 ounces) crushed tomatoes in purée
1½ cups uncooked elbow macaroni
2 tablespoons *French's*® Worcestershire Sauce
1 cup shredded Cheddar cheese
1½ cups *French's*® French Fried Onions

1. Cook meat in large nonstick skillet over medium-high heat until browned and no longer pink; drain.

2. Add tomatoes, macaroni and *1½ cups water*. Bring to boiling. Boil, partially covered, 10 minutes until macaroni is tender. Stir in Worcestershire.

3. Sprinkle with cheese and French Fried Onions.

Makes 6 servings

Tip: For a Southwestern flavor, add 2 tablespoons chili powder to ground beef and substitute 2 tablespoons *Frank's*® RedHot Sauce for the Worcestershire.

Spicy Quick and Easy Chili

Soups, Stews & Chilis

Taco Soup

½ pound ground beef
1 cup chopped onion
1 can (16 ounces) pinto beans in Mexican-style sauce
1 can (about 14 ounces) stewed tomatoes, undrained
1 can (10 ounces) diced tomatoes and green chiles
2 teaspoons chili powder
5 (8-inch) corn tortillas
  Nonstick cooking spray
5 cups shredded iceberg lettuce
½ cup shredded sharp Cheddar cheese
¼ cup chopped fresh cilantro (optional)

1. Preheat oven to 350°F. Spray large saucepan with nonstick cooking spray. Heat over medium-high heat until hot. Add beef and onion. Brown beef 6 to 8 minutes, stirring to break up meat. Drain fat. Add beans, stewed tomatoes with juice, diced tomatoes and chili powder. Bring to a boil. Reduce heat to low. Cover and simmer 10 minutes.

2. Place tortillas on baking sheet. Spray tortillas lightly on both sides with cooking spray. Using pizza cutter, cut each tortilla into 6 wedges. Bake 5 minutes.

3. Divide lettuce equally among soup bowls. Ladle beef mixture over lettuce. Top with cheese and cilantro, if desired. Serve with tortilla wedges. *Makes 5 servings*

Prep and Cook Time: 25 minutes

Wild Rice Soup

½ cup uncooked wild rice
1 pound lean ground beef
1 can (14½ ounces) chicken broth
1 can (10¾ ounces) condensed cream of mushroom soup
2 cups milk
1 cup (4 ounces) shredded Cheddar cheese
⅓ cup shredded carrot
1 package (0.4 ounce) HIDDEN VALLEY® The Original Ranch®
    Buttermilk Recipe Salad Dressing Mix
Chopped green onions with tops

Cook rice according to package directions to make about 1½ cups cooked rice. In Dutch oven or large saucepan, brown beef; drain off excess fat. Stir in rice, chicken broth, cream of mushroom soup, milk, cheese, carrot and dry salad dressing mix. Heat to a simmer over low heat, stirring occasionally, about 15 minutes. Serve in warmed soup bowls; top with green onions. Garnish with additional green onions, if desired. *Makes 6 to 8 servings*

Texas Chili

4 tablespoons vegetable oil, divided
2 large onions, chopped
3 large cloves garlic, minced
2 pounds boneless sirloin or round steak, cut into ½-inch cubes
1 pound ground beef
2 cans (16 ounces each) tomatoes in purée
1 can (15 to 19 ounces) red kidney beans, undrained
⅓ cup *Frank's® RedHot®* Cayenne Pepper Sauce
¼ cup chili powder
2 tablespoons ground cumin
1 tablespoon dried oregano leaves
½ teaspoon ground black pepper

1. Heat 1 tablespoon oil in 5-quart saucepan or Dutch oven. Add onions and garlic; cook 5 minutes or until tender. Transfer to small bowl; set aside.

2. Heat remaining 3 tablespoons oil in saucepan. Add sirloin and ground beef in batches; cook about 15 minutes or until well browned. Drain off fat.

3. Stir in remaining ingredients. Bring to a boil over medium-high heat. Return onions and garlic to saucepan. Simmer, partially covered, 1 hour or until meat is tender. Garnish with shredded Cheddar cheese and chopped green onion, if desired.   *Makes 10 servings*

Prep Time: 15 minutes
Cook Time: 1 hour 20 minutes

Quick Beef Soup

1½ pounds lean ground beef
1 cup chopped onion
2 cloves garlic, finely chopped
1 can (28 ounces) tomatoes, undrained
6 cups water
6 beef bouillon cubes
¼ teaspoon black pepper
1½ cups frozen peas, carrots and corn vegetable blend
½ cup uncooked orzo
French bread (optional)

Cook beef, onion and garlic in large saucepan over medium-high heat until beef is brown, stirring to separate meat; drain fat.

Purée tomatoes with juice in covered blender or food processor. Add tomatoes with juice, water, bouillon cubes and pepper to meat mixture. Bring to a boil; reduce heat to low. Simmer, uncovered, 20 minutes. Add vegetables and orzo. Simmer 15 minutes more. Serve with French bread. *Makes 6 servings*

*Favorite recipe from **North Dakota Beef Commission***

Chili with Chocolate

    1 pound ground beef
    1 medium onion, chopped
    3 cloves garlic, minced, divided
    1 can (28 ounces) diced tomatoes, undrained
    1 can (15 ounces) chili beans
 1½ tablespoons chili powder
    1 tablespoon grated semisweet baking chocolate
 1½ teaspoons cumin
    Hot pepper sauce
    Salt and black pepper

SLOW COOKER DIRECTIONS

1. Brown ground beef, onion and 1 clove garlic in large nonstick skillet 6 to 8 minutes over medium-high heat, stirring to break up meat. Drain fat.

2. Place meat mixture in slow cooker. Add remaining ingredients, including 2 cloves garlic; mix well. Cover and cook on LOW 5 to 6 hours. Garnish as desired. *Makes 4 servings*

There's no need to peel cloves of garlic before putting them through a garlic press—the skins will stay behind in the press when the garlic cloves are forced through it.

Chili with Chocolate

Hearty Ground Beef Stew

1 pound ground beef
3 cloves garlic, minced
1 package (16 ounces) Italian-style frozen vegetables
2 cups Southern-style hash brown potatoes
1 jar (14 ounces) marinara sauce
1 can (10½ ounces) condensed beef broth
3 tablespoons *French's®* Worcestershire Sauce

Brown beef with garlic in large saucepan; drain. Add remaining ingredients. Heat to boiling. Cover. Reduce heat to medium-low. Cook 10 minutes or until vegetables are crisp-tender. Serve in warm bowls with garlic bread, if desired. *Makes 6 servings*

Quick & Easy Chili

1 pound ground beef
1 medium onion, chopped
2 cloves garlic, finely chopped
2 cans (15 ounces each) kidney, pinto or black beans, drained
1 jar (16 ounces) ORTEGA® SALSA (any flavor)
1 can (4 ounces) ORTEGA® Diced Green Chiles
2 teaspoons chili powder
½ teaspoon dried oregano, crushed
½ teaspoon ground cumin
  Topping suggestions: ORTEGA® SALSA, shredded Cheddar or Monterey Jack cheese, chopped tomatoes, sliced ripe olives, sliced green onions and sour cream

COOK beef, onion and garlic in large skillet over medium-high heat for 4 to 5 minutes or until beef is no longer pink; drain.

STIR in beans, salsa, chiles, chili powder, oregano and cumin. Bring to a boil. Reduce heat to low; cook, covered, for 20 to 25 minutes.

TOP as desired before serving. *Makes 6 servings*

Meaty Chili

1 pound coarsely ground beef
¼ pound ground Italian sausage
1 large onion, chopped
2 medium ribs celery, diced
2 fresh jalapeño peppers,* chopped
2 cloves garlic, minced
1 can (28 ounces) whole peeled tomatoes, undrained, cut up
1 can (15 ounces) pinto beans, drained
1 can (12 ounces) tomato juice
1 cup water
¼ cup ketchup
1 teaspoon sugar
1 teaspoon chili powder
½ teaspoon salt
½ teaspoon ground cumin
½ teaspoon dried thyme
⅛ teaspoon black pepper

Jalapeño peppers can sting and irritate the skin; wear rubber gloves when handling peppers and do not touch eyes.

1. Cook beef, sausage, onion, celery, jalapeños and garlic in 5-quart Dutch oven over medium-high heat until meat is browned and onion is tender, stirring frequently.

2. Stir in tomatoes with juice, beans, tomato juice, water, ketchup, sugar, chili powder, salt, cumin, thyme and black pepper. Bring to a boil over high heat. Reduce heat to medium-low; simmer, uncovered, 30 minutes, stirring occasionally.

3. Ladle into bowls. Garnish as desired.   *Makes 6 servings*

In a
FLASH

Beefy Bean & Walnut Stir-Fry

1 teaspoon vegetable oil
3 cloves garlic, minced
1 pound lean ground beef
1 bag (16 ounces) BIRDS EYE® frozen Cut Green Beans,
   thawed
1 teaspoon salt
½ cup walnut pieces

• In large skillet, heat oil and garlic over medium heat
about 30 seconds.

• Add beef and beans; sprinkle with salt. Mix well.

• Cook 5 minutes or until beef is browned, stirring
occasionally.

• Stir in walnuts; cook 2 minutes more.

Makes 4 servings

Serving Suggestion: Serve over hot cooked egg noodles
or rice.

Fast 'n Easy Chili

  1½ **pounds ground beef**
   1 **envelope LIPTON® RECIPE SECRETS® Onion Soup Mix***
   1 **can (15 to 19 ounces) red kidney or black beans, drained**
  1½ **cups water**
   1 **can (8 ounces) tomato sauce**
   4 **teaspoons chili powder**

*Also terrific with LIPTON® RECIPE SECRETS® Beefy Mushroom, Onion-Mushroom or Beefy Onion Soup Mix.

1. In 12-inch skillet, brown ground beef over medium-high heat; drain.

2. Stir in remaining ingredients. Bring to a boil over high heat. Reduce heat to low and simmer covered, stirring occasionally, 20 minutes. Serve, if desired, over hot cooked rice.

Makes 6 servings

First Alarm Chili: Add 5 teaspoons chili powder.

Second Alarm Chili: Add 2 tablespoons chili powder.

Third Alarm Chili: Add chili powder at your own risk.

Crunchy Layered Beef & Bean Salad

1 pound ground beef
2 cans (15 to 19 ounces *each***) black beans or pinto beans, rinsed**
and drained
1 can (14½ ounces) stewed tomatoes, undrained
1⅓ cups *French's*® **French Fried Onions, divided**
1 tablespoon *Frank's*® *RedHot*® **Cayenne Pepper Sauce**
1 package (1¼ ounces) taco seasoning mix
6 cups shredded lettuce
1 cup (4 ounces) shredded Cheddar or Monterey Jack cheese

1. Cook beef in large nonstick skillet over medium heat until thoroughly browned; drain well. Stir in beans, tomatoes, ⅔ *cup* French Fried Onions, *Frank's RedHot* Sauce and taco seasoning. Heat to boiling. Cook over medium heat 5 minutes, stirring occasionally.

2. Spoon beef mixture over lettuce on serving platter. Top with cheese.

3. Microwave remaining ⅔ *cup* onions 1 minute on HIGH. Sprinkle over salad. *Makes 6 servings*

Prep Time: 10 minutes
Cook Time: 6 minutes

Quick Chunky Chili

1 pound ground beef
1 medium onion, chopped
1 tablespoon chili powder
1½ teaspoons ground cumin
2 cans (16 ounces each) diced tomatoes, undrained
1 can (15 ounces) pinto beans, drained
½ cup prepared salsa
½ cup shredded Cheddar cheese
3 tablespoons sour cream
4 teaspoons sliced black olives

1. Brown beef and onion in 3-quart saucepan 6 to 8 minutes over medium-high heat, stirring to break up meat. Drain fat.

2. Add chili powder and cumin; stir 1 minute or until fragrant. Add tomatoes, beans and salsa. Bring to a boil; stir constantly. Reduce heat to low, simmer, covered, 10 minutes.

3. Top with cheese, sour cream and olives.   *Makes 4 servings*

Taco Taters

1 pound ground beef
1 jar (26 to 28 ounces) RAGÚ® Old World Style® Pasta Sauce
1 package (1.25 ounces) taco seasoning mix
6 large all-purpose potatoes, unpeeled and baked

1. In 12-inch skillet, brown ground beef over medium-high heat; drain. Stir in Ragú Pasta Sauce and taco seasoning mix and cook 5 minutes.

2. To serve, cut a lengthwise slice from top of each potato. Evenly spoon beef mixture onto each potato. Garnish, if desired, with shredded Cheddar cheese and sour cream.   *Makes 6 servings*

Prep Time: 5 minutes
Cook Time: 15 minutes

Quick Chunky Chili

In a Flash

Ranchero Onion Burgers

  1 pound ground beef
  ½ cup salsa
  ½ cup (2 ounces) shredded Monterey Jack cheese
1⅓ cups *French's*® French Fried Onions, divided
  ½ teaspoon garlic powder
  ¼ teaspoon ground black pepper
  4 hamburger rolls

Combine beef, salsa, cheese, ⅔ *cup* French Fried Onions, garlic powder and pepper in large bowl. Shape into 4 patties.

Place patties on oiled grid. Grill* over medium coals 10 minutes or until no longer pink in center, turning once. Serve on rolls. Garnish with additional salsa, if desired. Top with remaining ⅔ *cup* onions.

Makes 4 servings

*Or, broil 6 inches from heat.

Tip: For extra-crispy warm onion flavor, heat French Fried Onions in the microwave for 1 minute. Or, place in foil pan and heat on the grill 2 minutes.

Prep Time: 10 minutes
Cook Time: 10 minutes

Salisbury Steaks with Mushroom-Wine Sauce

1 pound ground beef
¾ teaspoon garlic salt or seasoned salt
¼ teaspoon black pepper
2 tablespoons butter or margarine
1 package (8 ounces) sliced button mushrooms *or* 2 packages
  (4 ounces each) sliced exotic mushrooms
2 tablespoons sweet vermouth or ruby port wine
1 jar (12 ounces) *or* 1 can (10½ ounces) beef gravy

1. Heat large heavy nonstick skillet over medium-high heat 3 minutes or until hot.* Meanwhile, combine ground beef, garlic salt and pepper; mix well. Shape mixture into four ¼-inch-thick oval patties.

2. Place patties in skillet; cook 3 minutes per side or until browned. Transfer to plate. Pour off drippings.

3. Melt butter in skillet; add mushrooms. Cook and stir 2 minutes. Add vermouth; cook 1 minute. Add gravy; mix well.

4. Return patties to skillet; simmer uncovered over medium heat 2 minutes for medium or until desired doneness, turning meat and stirring sauce. *Makes 4 servings*

If pan is not heavy, use medium heat.

Note: For a special touch, sprinkle steaks with chopped parsley or chives.

Prep and Cook Time: 20 minutes

Speedy Beef & Bean Burritos

8 (7-inch) flour tortillas
1 pound ground beef
1 cup chopped onion
1 teaspoon minced garlic
1 can (15 ounces) black beans, drained and rinsed
1 cup spicy thick and chunky salsa
2 teaspoons ground cumin
1 bunch cilantro
2 cups (8 ounces) shredded cojack or Monterey Jack cheese

1. Preheat oven to 350°F. Wrap tortillas in foil; place on center rack in oven. Heat tortillas 15 minutes.

2. Meanwhile, brown beef, onion and garlic in large skillet 6 to 8 minutes over medium-high heat, stirring to break up meat. Drain fat.

3. Stir beans, salsa and cumin into beef mixture; reduce heat to medium. Cover and simmer 10 minutes, stirring once.

4. Meanwhile, chop enough cilantro to measure ¼ cup. Stir into filling. Spoon filling down centers of warm tortillas; top with cheese. Roll up and serve immediately.   *Makes 4 servings*

Prep and Cook Time: 20 minutes

Speedy Beef & Bean Burritos

Joe's Special

1 pound ground beef
2 cups sliced mushrooms
1 small chopped onion
2 teaspoons Worcestershire sauce
1 teaspoon dried oregano
1 teaspoon ground nutmeg
½ teaspoon garlic powder
½ teaspoon salt
1 package (10 ounces) frozen chopped spinach, thawed
4 eggs, lightly beaten
⅓ cup grated Parmesan cheese

1. Spray large skillet with nonstick cooking spray. Brown beef, mushrooms and onion 6 to 8 minutes over medium-high heat, stirring to break up meat. Drain fat. Add Worcestershire, oregano, nutmeg, garlic powder and salt.

2. Drain spinach (do not squeeze dry); stir into meat mixture. Push mixture to one side of pan. Reduce heat to medium. Pour eggs into other side of pan; cook, without stirring, 1 to 2 minutes or until set on bottom. Lift eggs to allow uncooked portion to flow underneath. Repeat until softly set. Gently stir into meat mixture and heat through. Stir in cheese. *Makes 4 to 6 servings*

Serving Suggestion: Serve with salsa and toast.

Prep and Cook Time: 20 minutes

Mini Mexican Burger Bites

1½ pounds ground beef
½ cup finely chopped red, yellow or green bell pepper
2 tablespoons *French's®* Worcestershire Sauce
1 teaspoon *Frank's® RedHot®* Cayenne Pepper Sauce
1 teaspoon dried oregano leaves
¼ teaspoon salt
12 mini dinner rolls
　Shredded Cheddar cheese

1. Gently combine all ingredients except rolls and cheese in large bowl. Shape into 12 mini patties. Broil or grill patties 4 to 6 minutes for medium doneness (160°F internal temperature), turning once.

2. Arrange burgers on rolls and top with Cheddar cheese. Top with shredded lettuce, if desired. *Makes 6 servings*

Tacos Olé

1 pound ground beef
1 cup salsa
¼ cup *Frank's® RedHot®* Cayenne Pepper Sauce
2 teaspoons chili powder
8 taco shells, heated
　Garnish: chopped tomatoes, shredded lettuce, sliced olives, sour cream, shredded cheese

1. Cook beef in skillet over medium-high heat 5 minutes or until browned, stirring to separate meat; drain. Stir in salsa, **Frank's RedHot** Sauce and chili powder. Heat to boiling. Reduce heat to medium-low. Cook 5 minutes, stirring often.

2. To serve, spoon meat mixture into taco shells. Splash on more **Frank's RedHot** Sauce to taste. Garnish as desired.
Makes 4 servings

In a Flash

BBQ Beef Pizza

½ **pound ground beef**
¾ **cup prepared barbecue sauce**
 1 **(14-inch) prepared pizza crust**
 3 **to 4 onion slices, separated into rings**
 1 **medium green bell pepper, seeded and cut into ¼-inch-thick rings**
½ **(2¼-ounce can) sliced black olives, drained**
 1 **cup (4 ounces) shredded Colby-Jack cheese**

1. Preheat oven to 400°F.

2. Brown beef in large skillet 6 to 8 minutes over medium-high heat, stirring to break up meat. Drain fat. Remove from heat and stir in barbecue sauce.

3. Place pizza crust on baking pan. Spread meat mixture over pizza crust to within ½ inch of edge. Arrange onion slices and pepper rings over meat. Sprinkle with olives and cheese. Bake 8 minutes or until cheese is melted. Cut into 8 wedges.   *Makes 3 to 4 servings*

Prep and Cook Time: 20 minutes

BBQ Beef Pizza

Spanish Skillet Supper

½ **pound ground beef**
1 **small onion, chopped**
2¼ **cups water**
  1 **cup frozen whole kernel corn, partially thawed**
  1 **tablespoon margarine or butter**
  1 **package LIPTON® Rice & Sauce—Spanish**
¼ **cup shredded Cheddar cheese (about 1 ounce) (optional)**

1. Brown ground beef and onion in 12-inch nonstick skillet over medium-high heat; drain. Remove and set aside.

2. Add water, corn, margarine and Rice & Sauce—Spanish and bring to a boil. Continue boiling over medium heat, stirring occasionally, 10 minutes or until rice is tender.

3. Stir in beef mixture; heat through. Sprinkle with cheese.

Makes about 2 servings

Corny Sloppy Joes

1 **pound lean ground beef**
1 **small onion, chopped**
1 **can (15½ ounces) sloppy joe sauce**
1 **box (10 ounces) BIRDS EYE® frozen Sweet Corn**
6 **hamburger buns**

• In large skillet, cook beef and onion over high heat until beef is well browned.

• Stir in sloppy joe sauce and corn; reduce heat to low and simmer 5 minutes or until heated through.

• Serve mixture in hamburger buns.   *Makes 6 servings*

Serving Suggestion: Sprinkle with shredded Cheddar cheese.

*The publisher would like to thank
the companies and organizations listed below
for the use of their recipes and photographs in this publication.*

Birds Eye®

Del Monte Corporation

The Golden Grain Company®

The Hidden Valley® Food Products Company

Lawry's® Foods, Inc.

McIlhenny Company (TABASCO® brand Pepper Sauce)

Nestlé USA

North Dakota Beef Commission

North Dakota Wheat Commission

Reckitt Benckiser

Riviana Foods Inc.

Unilever Bestfoods North America

Wisconsin Milk Marketing Board

Index

Index

METRIC CONVERSION CHART

VOLUME MEASUREMENTS (dry)

1/8 teaspoon = 0.5 mL
1/4 teaspoon = 1 mL
1/2 teaspoon = 2 mL
3/4 teaspoon = 4 mL
1 teaspoon = 5 mL
1 tablespoon = 15 mL
2 tablespoons = 30 mL
1/4 cup = 60 mL
1/3 cup = 75 mL
1/2 cup = 125 mL
2/3 cup = 150 mL
3/4 cup = 175 mL
1 cup = 250 mL
2 cups = 1 pint = 500 mL
3 cups = 750 mL
4 cups = 1 quart = 1 L

VOLUME MEASUREMENTS (fluid)

1 fluid ounce (2 tablespoons) = 30 mL
4 fluid ounces (1/2 cup) = 125 mL
8 fluid ounces (1 cup) = 250 mL
12 fluid ounces (1 1/2 cups) = 375 mL
16 fluid ounces (2 cups) = 500 mL

WEIGHTS (mass)

1/2 ounce = 15 g
1 ounce = 30 g
3 ounces = 90 g
4 ounces = 120 g
8 ounces = 225 g
10 ounces = 285 g
12 ounces = 360 g
16 ounces = 1 pound = 450 g

DIMENSIONS

1/16 inch = 2 mm
1/8 inch = 3 mm
1/4 inch = 6 mm
1/2 inch = 1.5 cm
3/4 inch = 2 cm
1 inch = 2.5 cm

OVEN TEMPERATURES

250°F = 120°C
275°F = 140°C
300°F = 150°C
325°F = 160°C
350°F = 180°C
375°F = 190°C
400°F = 200°C
425°F = 220°C
450°F = 230°C

BAKING PAN SIZES

Utensil	Size in Inches/Quarts	Metric Volume	Size in Centimeters
Baking or Cake Pan (square or rectangular)	8×8×2	2 L	20×20×5
	9×9×2	2.5 L	23×23×5
	12×8×2	3 L	30×20×5
	13×9×2	3.5 L	33×23×5
Loaf Pan	8×4×3	1.5 L	20×10×7
	9×5×3	2 L	23×13×7
Round Layer Cake Pan	8×1½	1.2 L	20×4
	9×1½	1.5 L	23×4
Pie Plate	8×1¼	750 mL	20×3
	9×1¼	1 L	23×3
Baking Dish or Casserole	1 quart	1 L	—
	1½ quart	1.5 L	—
	2 quart	2 L	—